TENDER

✿

TENDER

✺

SARAH BATES

NEW MICHIGAN PRESS
TUCSON, ARIZONA

NEW MICHIGAN PRESS
DEPT OF ENGLISH, P. O. BOX 210067
UNIVERSITY OF ARIZONA
TUCSON, AZ 85721-0067

<http://newmichiganpress.com>

Orders and queries to <nmp@thediagram.com>.

ISBN 978-1-934834-74-5. FIRST PRINTING.

Design by Ander Monson.

Cover image courtesy of the author.

CONTENTS

FOXFIRE

I should have known when he sent me
the kissy face. *Maybe the point is not
to choose.* There is a poem in the desert
and there is a bike in the middle of it.
I can't see it, but it's there above the red
cliffs, the blue paint, hunters moving
fast toward primary colors. I still don't
know what to do with all these bones.
I remember the bee dying one afternoon
in between the lime green cushion
and rotting wood. My friend was there
and I didn't cry for two days. What
I remember most was you stopping
to pick up the piece of broken kindling
to tell a story of ecosystems, this extinct
fungus glowing on the red rocks. I get so
tired of men asking me for a blowjob
over coffee. I want a helicopter to fly over
and to know that it's there. I want the bee
to move one of its wings in the middle
of the oil slick and for the blue paint
to scatter. I want to see your grocery lists
in book spines, the desert sky, in knowing
that all things end. I want to be the bike
that is hard for colonists to reach, to be
leaving, always leaving. Months later,

a student writes, muscles are some of
the first organs broken down, and the most
important muscle in the body is the heart.
I should have known that in order to take
from the body, you have to give to the body.
I should have known that I was only building
a small empire to put things on.

MADAGASCAR

I'm watching the second episode of *Planet Earth* when he finally messages back, *earthy colors are great!* This is the part in early spring where the hatchling emerges, vulnerable. This is the part where the Himalayan snow leopard adapts its body and its behavior in order to survive. My mother keeps telling me to download a dating app in order to join the others at sea. I can't hear her over the snakes missing their chance, more baby iguanas finding their way onto the flat ground. Because I, too, want a little corner of Madagascar to myself. I, too, want to be like everyone else at 27 who seems to be getting on with it. Part of the reason why I love the color blue is because it is always letting our bodies go towards the way of our fears. Like men studying rats, bees gathering the tops of mulberry trees in order to dispose of them. Last night I allowed the ants to teach me something new about the waxing gibbous, a shadowy peace asserting itself like a person. I never told you how I had to stop in the middle of Highway 56 to see the dead coyote in the gutter, to bury its milk jaw, its gun-broke hip joint. I knew you had never seen pictures of the Falling Springs in October, the baby iguana outrunning a racer for the second time. I knew that in the last five minutes the seeds would disperse and the danger would be gone. The pressure of growth is in every part of every living thing.

EMILY DICKINSON DIDN'T HAVE A BOYFRIEND

Now when I think of it, I'm not sure
why he talks to me, this morning
he tagged me in a post about fungi
and I am suddenly an amateur
mycologist—I call up Gary Lincoff
and now we are walking around
Central Park holding up signs of tiny
yellow mushrooms: *FUNGI FOR
THE PEOPLE!* I tell myself: I can go
hunt for it if I like—this morning
while he slept, I watched the spiders
beside the microwave bursting
like orange poppies, a small army
splitting across highways, creeks
draining towns of small fish I walked
down to the canyon and the children
everywhere becoming bees, becoming
burnt hot dogs, nuclei flowing freely
against the mountains, I went home
and washed the vase: I am always
letting the beast do whatever he wants
everywhere I go it's always the biggest
mushroom I've ever seen I tell him:
let's find a hot spring somewhere up
North and make out *is there anything
better than being in water with the one you*

love now when I think of it, I am always
doing things I don't want to do he sends
me a picture of baby avocados drowning
in the blue water, I tell him: I think I have
vascular wilt disease, imagine an entire log
spilling germinate green onto I-70 this
morning I am flying to the Douglas-fir
to lay eggs and die now when I think
of it, it's the female who goes first,
limping with both feet

CHRISTMAS BIRD COUNT

Bird enthusiasts might call it inhaling
the spore, the way I study the wound
and read about nature. The nest of
goldfinches reminded me of the nervous
system of a pigeon, the portrait
of the boy holding a shell to his ear
asking about the cries of killdeers. I'm sure
there are other moons, more beaches.
A color to describe the part of the frog's
hind leg where the snake finds its way in.
This year the head of the James settling
at my feet, you sitting on top of the rocks
counting 78 different species, two eastern
towhees foraging on a small patch of white.
I know I was wrong to say whether it was
a hemlock or a sycamore, I know I was wrong
to believe that the rains would come again
and take the old tree with it. In many birds,
the beak is the only organ capable of being
grasped. In order to understand the life
of any animal, you try to get answers. Call it
transparent walls, a stranger passing in the
crosswalk, call this the feeling of Antarctica
breaking off and not being able to name it.

OH, MOTHER ELK

I have told no one what I did in the backseat
    of your truck. I have said nothing
to the roofs of my heart about the pregnant elk

looking up at the Patriarchs— a story of animals
    turning to bones in the dark. I was standing
on the side of the road in Toquerville throwing up

this whole summer, a gallon of water, the gut pile
    and its partial hide
found somewhere in between the Virgin River

and an orange flower. I thought that if I spoke
    to you of the soft-bodied mother,
twelve-year-old boys knocking over half a million

hives, a sun who takes the fish out of its own skin.
    I thought if I spoke to you of another star
system, my father's eyes, if you let me speak to you

of heaven even if it doesn't exist— you would know
    what it was like to open my body to it, to boil
water. How this world keeps me from my own grief.

Even in the mountains where you first took me, I am
    thinking of the herd of fifty-seven elk and all
the men shooting, the librarians delivering books on

horseback. My species only wanting to become
the flowers themselves, the last living thing
she saw. I love how I am always starting over.

TYRANNY, LIKE HELL

1 / the heart   viewed from space,   tramples beetles   without

knowing.   I get so tired of the successful   sun,   another container

drunk   off creation.   maybe   I'm walking across   Yankee Meadows

trying   to keep others away. if i search   through its stomach

always wanting   an occasion for home, perhaps somewhere

in my body   2 / I wanted   to die   in the canyon   where sandstone

fades.   for miles   i'd shout   at the squid   used as bait,

the coyote's hips   hanging   from the juniper tree.   *on this day*

in history,   *men erased moons,*   then drew pictures   of the Queen

herself   with the velvet of its antlers,   imagine this: the moon

half-moving,   half-dead mistaking   comets   for sea monsters,

someone else's sun   for another hour   spent   cleaning

off the bone.   maybe   I   3 / was wrong to say Zion, maybe a Queen   would have   looked up at Mars   and believed.

from here,   everything holds colors.   from the top of   Angel's

Landing   to the curve   of Blue Ridge,   the blood

in my hands settles into the rocks,   and then   I leave.

YOUR EARTH IS ONE TINY NEIGHBORHOOD

what I want is a little more
    Apollo,

give me a muck of stars,
    a river of half ocean sleeping,

Sudan kissing the tops of my knees
    while I teach the white ants to scatter

studies show that months after we dropped
    the bomb, barn swallows would spend hours

collecting teeth, rotting telescopes, *was that your heart*
    or was it mine?

no matter how much I want your Earth to stay,
    it goes

tonight the guy across town wants me to touch myself
    and think of him,

I wonder what the elk does with its antlers when the forest
    catches fire,

do female termites in Japan really need male termites in order
    to make baby termites?

I keep trying to forget that episode of *Friends* where the lobsters
    mate for life, but there it is buried in the frozen lake,

sunk beneath the swallow's blue nest, up until the barred owls
    came back for their eggs, everything was mine.

Because while the male is making up his mind,

the female speaks of a season so suddenly green,
        the city lit up flying saucer small

because at first glance, ants seem to treat their dead
    the same way as humans,

the body untouched for days,
    whenever the moon falls back to sleep, I touch

myself   until the stars hurt all over

QUICKENING, I READ ABOUT THE CLAM'S HEART

in the dream / the bears / are actual bears / the bears are big /
and brown / the bears / are angry / i'm guessing the bears in the
dream are grizzlies/because in the dream / I do not run / from
the bears / in the dream / i know / that the bears are coming /
for me / but in the dream / the bears stop / for anything / that
has been lost / between my body / and the blue sky / this part
is strange the bears / stopping for a tree / that has lost its leaves
/ the dark colored kidney / of a clam / its heart / in the dream I
know / that the bears / are not actual bears / one of the effects
/ of pain / is we have to / reckon with the body

NOT ANOTHER DEAD WHALE POEM

All my friends want a happy ending / another dead whale is
like another dead sea /

another mountain that got separated from its mother and
starved to death

why don't you write a poem about *Free Willy* instead /

doesn't he jump over the wall at the end?

one friend says another dead whale is just another dead
boyfriend who after six months ghosted

and I sort of agree /

from water to rainforest I never sleep anymore

I Google dead whale in Utah /

dead whale found on a farm by the Great Salt Lake /

whale bones found in the Egyptian desert and now all I can
think about is Pharaoh's body

found somewhere beside the deadliness of a 65-foot whale /

perhaps none of these things

ever even happened /

when they found the whale in thick shrubs and coral getting
picked apart by vultures /

and when they found it in a field of orange poppies while
searching for a lost cow

Fox 13 Now called the story "Davis County has a whale of a tale
on its hands"

I didn't want another whale to be dead /

they say the whale was too large

in too remote of an area to be entirely removed /

they imagine it was floating without thinking

and then the tide took it far into the mangrove /

I imagine it only wanted the deep warm face of water

the sky to be seen from everywhere /

I didn't want the whale to be dead

I only wanted my mother to call me one morning / just to weep

RAINBOW BRIDGE

The first time we held hands, I rushed home to read Barthes.
In reality, it was only September, the parking lot of a fast food
Mexican restaurant that used to be a Wendy's. We never spoke,

in the way that junipers never speak, or the way in which holiness
is transported across time, hours confused by 1,960 miles
of shoreline. "I am mad to be in love," he begins on page 120,

"I am not mad to be able to say so." In my body, I knew it was
the brightest blue carrying us beyond the many reincarnations
of withoutness. I knew that when scientists came out with reports

of a second moon, it would be ours. My right thumb told me
I was through with not enough, how your elbows woke me that
Sunday morning and I was ready for all the delights of the earth.

That night, I searched your body from timezones away and finally
there was an end to my grief. Love has made me a madman
in the mountains, a tiny boat moving slowly down the Colorado

River. Finally it is midwinter and I am only here to pick flowers
from a frozen stream.

AFTER WHICH THE MALE DIES

for the thousandth time, I know I am not a queen
my mother says she had no idea how useful they were:

bees gathering nectar so deep in many flowers that some
cannot use their mouths to obtain it. like the bees,

I have used my mouth to gather love, a species, the moonlit
world in which I never get let in. Like the bees, I have

used my mouth to drag down the moose in the wild white
of winter, my teeth too worn to be useful. by the time

I was ready to peel back the bark of the jack pine, I squished
the tiny black beetle with my bare hands, the forest already

dead. it was the bees who told me of this royal jelly made
from the head glands of my daughters. for the thousandth

time, I have hovered over the blossom so long all I know
is that once a bee has drunk from the body of Saturn,

it returns again and again I am no fish, no wife, if I were
a queen I would make a hive out of the moon staying put,

I would mate with the male again and again just to watch
him die

FIELD MUSEUM

The woolly mammoth had to survive
off something. And the hanged moon
must have cried when the balloons
of triceratops finally floated upstream.

So what if I sort the silence of valley
floors, the long tusks of boars curving
back and down until they pierce confused

jaw. So what if I got my teeth into his skin
long enough to look inward. Would a whale
ever forget my favorite flower?

Dear love, I would like to follow you
to a field with a very yellow tent
and sleep there.

ASTRAGALUS

Everywhere the animals are dying   the flowers in Zion   bloom
    just to kill   The men in Utah want to keep   the wolves

out of Taylor Creek so they do   Maybe the Earth is running out
    of ochre   Maybe the desert   stars are more brilliant

in winter   Once, an elk brought down a helicopter   east of here
    and for hours   I dreamt   of the roaming smoke

The rings of Saturn desperate   to be touched Take for instance
    the black widow caught in the blue   and yellow strings

of the doormat   Its red belly pointed toward each phase
    of the moon   I have never been comfortable with beginnings

The sky still tender   with dead cows   a series of reddish dots
    flattened in the sun   This morning I am eating in the ditches

I am spraying the outside of the house   with peppermint and citrus
    I am trying to do the things   that are meaningful to me

I used to think I would rather kill   than be killed   I used to watch
    the female   open up the chest cavity   while the male rested

behind her   I know I have to die a few times   before I can use both
    of my hands

I know I am also violent   and doing these things   out of fear

THE DINOSAURS THAT DIDN'T DIE

I have never left the fields of frozen
buffalo Sometimes a woman is so bound
up in the bobbing of caves, she cannot
pull close enough to the water for sound
I used to cry to the smell of Old Spice
while scrubbing the soap scum off shower
heads Once in line at a CVS, I picked up
the latest issue of *National Geographic* so I
wasn't buying a twelve pack of condoms
alone Like the first bird, I, too, have always
wanted to gouge the earth, the one with
the plumage on its wings setting off a series
of catastrophic events I want to get to the part
of the story where the planet is lying down
On page 78, in the passenger seat of your blue
Jeep, I read "The Dinosaurs That Didn't Die"
just to think of all the ways a person can be
kissed I am afraid of the places my body
will never go I want to be jaws bristling, claws
out, another solar system with sharp teeth
That night you fixed the little girl's bike chains,
I wanted to tell you about the man who used
my body to get to the place where the asteroid
hit, where most of the dinosaurs died I have
always felt in my body this deadliness in being
too quiet for too long Sometimes a woman

is afraid of the things that happen that keep
even the oldest birds silent Picasso was on
the cover and the girl at the cash register
laughed and said something like, "wild night?"

HANS WHO CLAIMS HE LOVES THE STARS AND SPACE

Do you really think I'm going to have sex with someone who doesn't believe in the second moon?

YELLOWSTONE 926F

la loba they call it, the place where the killing
thing left me to die. I pay ninety bucks for
a mule ride and hope I can bury what's left
of my body somewhere along this shadow
of the North Rim's light. why kill a wolf
walking through the snow? I am here killing
thing, at the top of Bright Angel Point telling
this guy I matched with somewhere in between
Southern Utah and here that we should kiss.
killing thing I am like flowers, I turn in whatever
direction the sun is offered. the guy from
Snoqualmie Pass wants to know if this is what
I chose or if this is just where I ended up. dear
reader, I was covered with them: apples and
strawberries, a committee of buzzards in search
of some greenish earth, my whole life—the desert
pawing at a tin can, the sound making a frozen
lake around my neck. whenever we say flower,
it doesn't matter the excuses of dogs, a woman
driving through New Mexico with a pistol in her
hand. and in me owls, and the old lake, the bacteria
that ate the bad sun. while Earth was making
canyons to clean trout, Saturn built another moon
as a way of understanding loss, as a way of being
important to men. this is what the color red means:
it is easier to imagine myself coyote, kicking the

children off with my hind leg. from desert to desert,
I am thrown away.

ANYWAY, THAT WAS THE SADDEST PART

I often confuse the dead horses
for trees. I say things like termites

care about the weather, or dark stars
will always find their way to empty

rooms. Anyway, the dead horses are real,
and the trees are real. Tonight a herd

of cattle is headed back toward the town
and now the river is real. The Mesopotamia

is real and the people in the town are real.
And when I saw pictures of the bighorn

sheep, I wanted them to be real so I searched
for the hands that drew them. And anyway,

the narwhal fighting off another narwhal
in order to catch its own breath is real,

and sometimes when I am in Vermont,
I go into the woods to hide from the holiness

of conclusion, and sometimes it is so real
I don't want to come out. Anyway, listen to me

nature is real. And when seal pups kiss, it is real
just like the time we got a hotel room halfway

in between where you sleep and where I sleep
just to kiss. That was real. And yes, I often confuse

kissing with love, but when we kissed, it was real,
the same way love when it is love is real. And

to describe the language of love is to describe
the language of bees and that is to be real

and to buy something in order to remember
the describing and the kissing and the bees

is to be real. And anyway, on my way home,
I paid seventeen dollars for a piece of petrified

wood somewhere in between the kissing
and the describing and Holbrook, Arizona

and it felt so real that I called my mom just to talk
about the levels of brightness when two fighting

narwhals kiss. And anyway, I, too, want to be real.
Like spring, like swamps and like seaweed, I want

to see a whale from a beach town in California
or Rhode Island and to know that it's real.

Because when you touched me for the first time
I knew my body was real. The Mesopotamia

was there and the Tigris and the Euphrates
and for hours the bees crawled into the craters

of me as if my body had never been clawed into.
And because when I sent you the poem about

the dying whale, you wrote back, *why couldn't you
have the whale getting saved by a narwhal or something?*

Anyway, that was the saddest part.

WINSLOW CRATER

the sun could explode again, and the Wasatch
Mountains wanting water, would finally rip up
maps of the sunburnt tourists crawling out
of the hills, the fish dying slowly and then all
at once. the California condors will give what's
left of the river to sharks, and the moon tired
of picnickers and parachutes will paint the
smallest mule deer, shy, and falling from cliffs.
today I learned that clams have hearts so now
I can't stop picturing them driving around in
station wagons, baby clams wearing neon green
bathing caps, strawberry sunglasses. it only
takes a day to love someone. so I loved the rain:
too little or too much. I loved the gravitational
pull of rabbits drinking at a waterhole north
of Vegas. I loved standing over the crater in
Arizona imagining Tom Hanks in a space suit
and the clam's heart planting a flag on the moon's
bare, bright head. It struck me, the hippies
dancing, the golden fields of Vietnam replaced
by a turkey vulture and blown away, the tiny speck
where you once gave me laughter, and the next
day, the laughter killed me.

CONCERNING THE COYOTE

Concerning the coyote, I am lost
forever. I am weeping in the shower,
over the blueberries,

a deer that's been eaten
from the inside. To redirect your thoughts,
focus on what doesn't die. Shells,

like shoulders of dogwood, pits of ocean.
A meteor passing over a thousand pines
just to choose a mountain tired from

overgrown power lines. Fire is making
me aware of the roadkill. Fire is making me
responsible for my own restlessness.

Fire has become a British lord, replying strictly
in economic terms. Concerning the coyote,
I would have made for you and made for you

and made for you.

MISSED CONNECTION

In the town where the mayor sends a Facebook message To
warn the people of the wandering polar bear, I let you go. And
on page 105 of the *Brooklyn Rail*, a stranger named Emily writes
"Goodbye #4" so I guess this is goodbye to the wind, to the
branches and the boats moving through the Arctic Circle, you
in a pair of women's Bermuda shorts walking down the Las
Vegas strip alone. I hate the spring, the drought of every atom.
This is the aftermath of using a telescope in the middle of the
street for the second time. Another moon poem, but with birds,
birds flying over the red building, the river: another first date,
but you're on Earth and I'm on the moon. And yes, I've already
matched with someone new, but if you know anything about
the lines on a face, or the truth of a thing, you know that he
doesn't make me laugh like you. This morning, everyone at the
breakfast table is in love. And the sun is hard and the sentence
is soft and the people at the breakfast table are kind and now I
know how everything that is made can be broken. Like colors
painted on wood or skis made of glass. For weeks, I wanted to
text you from the Grand Canyon, "I think my heart is dying,"
but instead, I put it in a poem. Now I know how it sounds to
get from Bright Angel's Point to the wound. This is the 84,000
holes of my body, this is where the wind burns its tongue on its
own wailing. This is the trees looking back at the landscape in
order to move on.

FIFTY YEARS AFTER APOLLO 11

I'm sorry but the moon can go fuck itself
I am tired of all its waning
This phase of yellow dust and that
Suddenly the moth's enormous wings
Are a moon who does whatever it wants
Think of it in terms of junkyards piling up
My body turning green against rusting car parts
Plastic debris to quote Aldrin if we can see
The horizon we want to know what's beyond
When they landed I saw the shoreline
Of Lake Powell growing smaller above the clouds
I sat on the edge of the Mogollon Rim
In Arizona just to pass time
I'd rather have a dead Mars
Discovering Van Gogh for the first time
The penguins at the museum being carried off
On stretchers I'd like to hold a confused Saturn
Weeping over the six-week-old honeybee
Who needs a moon when you've got solar panels
Here are the facts: when the moon gets full
It is that feeling that something is there
Even though it's not
No the full moon is a call for forgiveness
That which wakes you in the middle of the night
I know this because I put the color blue
On a stick and held it at arm's length for 180 days

Hoping to hear from the other side
I know this because Buzz never strayed
More than 100 yards
And still he found a forest in between my body
And the suffering Yucca root
How many times must I leave orbit
To get to the beginning of my life
How many moons must I wait up for
So I can worship the fields instead
I know that when the sun and Earth meet
They vanish for Halloween I was a deer
My antlers down ready to charge

LET ME TELL YOU THIS ONCE

I am sick of the wolf snatching the daisy

History says soon everything will become
moonless

History says the truth is another river
swallowed up by the confused sea

No, I am sick of the wolf being called
a man

I keep translating water where there once
was water

I keep reaching for the dogwood's rotting
limbs because here it is always spring

For years I have translated the stars
because of the night sky

I've been trying to tell you that what I have
now is what I lost

History, cumulus and fat, has taught me
the face of a man refusing to get out

of the water because the water made him
feel good

Like poison oak, sometimes the moon
comes back and it is totally over

NODDING WILD ONION

When mathematicians use the word
    brush-footed, what they really mean
is: it went wrong for me from the beginning.

I turned the faucet on and the weeds
    were loaded with granite. I was coal
burning, rivers draining, ash sealed into centuries

old sandstone. I don't want pity, I don't want
    to speak. I want the bees to come with me
into the growling hills, the salmon to count

    the streams flooding with our own blood.
I want to nod like the wild onions nod at rainbows.
    At swamps. At the sunlight pouring in.

When God made the wolf, she did it in a stolen
    moment—without numbers, or sound, it was
snowing. *Rage, rage,* she said, to drill into my veins

this valley of unloved metal, to talk about the dirt
    being carried away from the Sonoran Desert
to the disassembling of wings, of softness, of air.

I am leaving so much of the science out of this.

READ ABOUT MY LIPS

I could make any waterfall
my killing ground

I could give away my body
as a noun or a field

a town full of baby whales
making a life

against purple canyons.
I could be mad about it

over and over again
or I could bring back the bees

with my own tears fill up
the streets with a hundred

pink moons. I am not lilies
or a metaphor for the man

who measured buffalo
falling from the sky

in Wyoming I am the god
of walking

of using my mouth
to make want

I could make the strawberries red
the constellations bleed

I could put the flowers
in a boat and listen to the wind

that sung while the stomach
of every star collapsed.

I have started to talk to my heart
like an old forest No more!

I could put on my yellow
boots and leave behind

every sky blue bowl

everything that is gone
I outlasted

YES, IT'S DISGUSTING WHEN YOU LOSE CONTROL

After Frank O'Hara

No matter how much you think you have been going with the
flow of Mount Kilauea, you can't get away from the whale that
washed up last week in Thailand. I am on one of those Choose
Your Own Adventures with the earth and I just ate eighty
garbage bags—in any case, the story begins where she goes
to drink water, and me: I wait for endings. The stone crushes
the man fleeing Pompeii, fire crosses the desert sky, the Pacific
ocean, Highway 93 while a mother grizzly feeds her youngest
cub a maple glazed donut. Infinity's a long ways away. LMNOP
is my favorite part of the song, TUV is that sad part, think
*this will help me learn the alphabet without having to sing it in
my head?* Sometimes when I am driving, "Fast Car" by Tracy
Chapman comes on and it gives me a weird feeling. It's my luck
I download a dating app, start bored swiping while on a family
vacation, and connect with someone I really enjoy talking to
that lives seven hours away. No regrets. I enjoy driving. *Did I
mention that you're very pretty?* Once, a guy told me it was my
fault that he tried to have sex with me after I told him I wasn't
going to have sex with him. It's your fault that you and your
nice lips came over and sat on my couch, he said, underneath
something framed that I swear looked just like a maple glazed
donut. Don't get me wrong, they're two of my favorite things,
making out and maple glazed donuts, but my body keeps telling
me I'm getting old and a few weeks ago, someone implied I'm

supposed to be someone who molds young minds. *Does someone who is supposed to mold young minds go over to a stranger's house on a school night just to make out and dream of donuts? Please meditate on how easily we accept women's pain as collateral damage in men's self-discovery.* No matter how much you think you have been going with the flow, you can't get away from the winter you watched Jaws 1, 2, and 3 a hundred times. In the past, I felt like my heart was too big, once, a 6'8 firefighter with a handlebar mustache, whose hobbies included french pressed coffee, Crossfit, and Tennessee Whiskey told me I was "to dam cute to be single." After so long, you get tired of keeping something in your throat that just won't go down. After so long, you get tired of peeling away your fear by munching on five-pound garbage bags. Last night I dreamt of the dying whale reciting its favorite part of the alphabet, and you seven hours away, eating a Kit Kat whole. I am on one of those Choose Your Own Adventures with the earth and I want you to come.

ACCORDING TO THE *FARMERS' ALMANAC*

I saw pictures of the blue whale's
heart and I cried. Nature is scary.
This morning I miss you because
of the sudden gunshot, a story
of wild horses piled up along
the rim waiting to die, all their
corsets of bone collecting dust
along the shores of a remote
island. What do I think of love?
The color of us dying was not sad
or unhappy, it made me unreal.
According to the *Farmers' Almanac*,
now is not the time for planting.
We take shelter at a hotel in between
Navajo water and Las Vegas;
we eat fried ice cream somewhere
in between the land of little rain
and man's desire to thrive. Everyone
wants to forget the suffering of birds.
How every mountain comes from
the mouth of an ocean. This morning
the baby whale has scratches on
its side from where it rubbed against
its mother. The night you left,
there was a telescope in the middle
of the street and all the children lined

up one after another hoping to get
a shot at the moon. Should I shout
into the gorge? Yell at the trees for not
gathering themselves? If there is fire
in the desert, it is here. If there is
a heart in the poem, it is mine.
According to the *Farmers' Almanac*,
people never know what they need
until it's given to them.

ACKNOWLEDGMENTS

"Madagascar," *The Boiler*, Fall 2019

"Yes, It's Disgusting When You Lose Control," "Fifty Years After Apollo." *Peach Magazine*, Summer 2019

"Oh, Mother Elk," "Quickening, I Read about the Clam's Heart," *Superstition Review*, Spring 2019,

"Anyway, That was the Saddest Part," *Hobart*, Spring 2019

"Emily Dickinson Didn't Have a Boyfriend," *DIAGRAM*, 2019

"After Which the Male Dies," *DIAGRAM*, 2019

"Let Me Tell You This Once," *RHINO*, Spring 2019

"According to the *Farmers' Almanac*," *BOOTH*, Spring 2019

"Tyranny, Like Hell," *Zone 3*, Spring 2019

"Foxfire," *Fugue*, Spring 2019

"Christmas Bird Count," *45th Parallel*, Summer 2018

SARAH BATES is from the Blue Ridge Mountains of Virginia. She has an MFA in Creative Writing from Northern Michigan University and currently teaches at Southern Utah University in Cedar City, Utah. Her work has appeared or is forthcoming in *Hotel Amerika*, *The Normal School*, *The Rumpus*, and *Seneca Review*, among others.

❉

COLOPHON

Text is set in a digital version of Jenson, designed by Robert Slimbach in 1996, and based on the work of punchcutter, printer, and publisher Nicolas Jenson. The titles here are in Futura.

＊

NEW MICHIGAN PRESS, based in Tucson, Arizona, prints poetry and prose chapbooks, especially work that transcends traditional genre. Together with DIAGRAM, NMP sponsors a yearly chapbook competition.

DIAGRAM, a journal of text, art, and schematic, is published bimonthly at THEDIAGRAM.COM. Periodic print anthologies are available from the New Michigan Press at NEWMICHIGANPRESS.COM.